W9-AWN-561

by Michael Sandler

Consultant: Charlie Zegers
Basketball Expert
basketball.about.com

New York, New York

Credits

Cover and Title Page, © Nathaniel S. Butler/NBAE via Getty Images, AP Photo/Nam Y. Huh, and Randy Belice/NBAE via Getty Images; 4, © AP Photo/Nam Y. Huh; 5, © John Gress/Reuters/ Landov; 6, © AP Photo/Charles Rex Arbogast; 7, © Dick Raphael/NBAE via Getty Images; 8, © Abel Uribe/Chicago Tribune; 9, © AP Photo/Brian Kersey; 10, © AP Photo/Mark Humphrey; 11, © AP Photo/Frank Franklin II; 12, © David E. Klutho/Sports Illustrated/Getty Images; 13, © Jeff Haynes/Reuters /Landov; 14, © AP Photo/Nam Y. Huh; 15, © Joe Skipper/Reuters/Landov; 16, © Michael J. LeBrecht II/Sports Illustrated/Getty Images; 17, © Randy Belice/NBAE via Getty Images; 18, © Christian Petersen/Getty Images; 19, © Gary Dineen/NBAE via Getty Images; 20, © Jonathan Daniel/Getty Images; 21, © Randy Belice/NBAE via Getty Images; 22R, © Chris Sweda/Chicago Tribune/MCT/Landov; 22L, © MCT/Newscom.

Publisher: Kenn Goin
Senior Editor: Lisa Wiseman
Creative Director: Spencer Brinker
Photo Researcher: We Research Pictures, LLC

Library of Congress Cataloging-in-Publication Data

Sandler, Michael, 1965-
  Derrick Rose / by Michael Sandler ; consultant, Charlie Zegers.
    p. cm. — (Basketball Heroes Making a Difference)
  Includes bibliographical references and index.
  ISBN-13: 978-1-61772-439-8 (library binding)
  ISBN-10: 1-61772-439-4 (library binding)
  1. Rose, Derrick—Juvenile literature. 2. Basketball players—United States—Biography—Juvenile literature. 3. African American basketball players—Biography—Juvenile literature. 4. Generosity—Juvenile literature. I. Zegers, Charlie. II. Title.
  GV884.R619S26 2012
  796.323092—dc23
  [B]
                              2011039985

For more information, write to Bearport Publishing Company, Inc., 45 West 21st Street, Suite 3B, New York, New York 10010. Printed in the United States of America.

10 9 8 7 6 5 4 3 2 1

Contents

Most Valuable Player

On May 4, 2011, the crowd at the United Center was cheering for its team—the Chicago Bulls. The loudest shouts were for Derrick Rose, the Bulls' homegrown star. He had just led Chicago to a big win over the Atlanta Hawks in the second game of the 2010–2011 **Eastern Conference** playoff series. Chicago had lost the first game, but Derrick, their quick and **agile point guard**, had used all his skills to help the team tie up the series.

The victory was the fans' second reason to applaud Derrick that night. Before the game started, NBA **commissioner** David Stern had presented Derrick with the Most Valuable Player (MVP) Award for the 2010–2011 season, the league's highest individual honor.

Fans at the United Center, home of the Chicago Bulls, show Derrick their support.

Derrick (#1) shoots the ball during the Bulls' 86–73 victory over the Hawks on May 4, 2011. The Bulls went on to win the playoff series four games to two.

At 22 years old, Derrick was the youngest NBA player ever to be named MVP.

Murray Park Hero

Before the playoff game on May 4, 2011, a crowd gathered at Murray Park in Chicago's Englewood neighborhood to celebrate Derrick's MVP award. Derrick had grown up in Englewood, and Murray Park was where he had learned the game.

It hadn't been easy to play basketball there, however. Players bumped up against one another hard. If someone got hit while **driving** the ball to the basket, no **foul** was called, even if it should have been. Bigger, older players never took it easy on the smaller, younger ones. Derrick, often the youngest player on the court, learned to twist his body in the air to avoid contact with other players. He also learned to make sure his shot went in, even if he got hit on the way to the hoop.

Murray Park, shown here, is about 13 miles (21 km) from the United Center.

Wilt Chamberlain (#13) during a game for the Philadelphia 76ers in 1968

Derrick was the first NBA player in more than 40 years to win the MVP award while playing for his hometown team. The only other player to do so was Hall of Fame center Wilt Chamberlain. Wilt was named MVP four times while playing in Philadelphia in the 1960s for the Warriors and the 76ers.

The Perfect Point Guard

As a child, nothing could keep Derrick away from basketball. "I used to live in that park," he remembers. He played all day, every day, refusing to stop when the sun went down even though the court had no lights. Once, he even showed up to play on the same day he had broken his arm while climbing a tree.

In middle school and high school, Derrick became an incredibly skilled player who took his position, point guard, very seriously. Although he could dunk easily as an eighth grader—unlike most of his friends—he didn't worry about scoring. To Derrick, his main job was throwing perfect passes to his open teammates.

Derrick playing basketball in high school

Derrick's love of passing made him very popular. "Everyone wanted to play with him," said one of his childhood basketball coaches.

Derrick played high school basketball for Chicago's Simeon Career Academy. In both his junior and senior years, he led Simeon to Illinois state **titles**. No public school team in Chicago had ever won back-to-back state championships before.

To Memphis, and Home!

Derrick was as surprised as everyone else with the success he had at such a young age. "I never thought I was that good," he recalled. By his senior year at Simeon, however, Derrick was so skilled that most people considered him the best high school player in the country. Dozens of colleges, including the University of Kansas and the University of Arizona, had tried to **recruit** him. These schools had some of the best basketball programs in the country.

Derrick chose to play at the University of Memphis. During his freshman year, his **accurate** passing and unstoppable scoring helped the Memphis Tigers reach the 2008 **NCAA Championship Game**. His one incredible college season showed that he was ready for the NBA, so in 2008, Derrick entered the NBA **draft**. With the number one pick, the Chicago Bulls naturally selected the country's number one college player—Derrick.

Derrick runs down the court during the 2008 NCAA Championship Game.

With Derrick playing point guard, Memphis won the first 26 games of the team's 2007–2008 season and finished with a 38–2 record. The 38 wins in the season were the most in NCAA history.

Derrick speaks to reporters after being selected by the Chicago Bulls in the 2008 draft.

Rookie Sensation

On draft day, a crowd gathered at Murray Park, the place where Derrick had played basketball as a child. His fans burst into cheers when they learned that Chicago had picked Derrick. The soon-to-be Bull was equally thrilled. Playing for his hometown team was like a dream come true.

Always **humble**, Derrick could hardly believe he had reached the NBA. Before his first preseason game, he stood on the court next to Dallas Mavericks **All-Star** Jason Kidd. "I never thought that I'd be playing against him," Derrick said. "I was shocked that I was even on the floor."

As a **rookie**, Derrick proved he belonged on the floor with NBA greats. He averaged nearly 17 points a game and had more than six **assists**. His passing and scoring earned him the 2008–2009 NBA Rookie of the Year Award.

Derrick (#1) attempts a shot against Jason Kidd during a game in 2008.

Derrick's second season with the Bulls was even better than his first. He was selected for the NBA All-Star Game, and capped off his year by starting for the U.S. team at the 2010 **FIBA World Championship**. Derrick helped lead Team USA to the gold medal.

Derrick (right) celebrates with his Team USA teammates after winning the gold medal.

Derrick's **humility** comes from his mother, Brenda. "She always told me that just because I can shoot a basketball better than someone else," he said, "I shouldn't think that I'm better than them."

Before his third NBA season began, however, Derrick surprised a group of reporters. Lacking his usual humility, he said, "Why can't I be MVP of the league?"

As it turned out, there was no reason why he couldn't. During the 2010–2011 season, he averaged 25 points a game with nearly 8 assists, and drastically improved his **outside shooting**. Most important, he led Chicago to the league's best record, 62–20. With all this success, the 22-year-old point guard did become the league MVP! While Derrick hadn't been humble, he turned out to have been right!

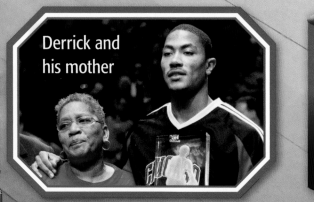

Derrick and his mother

Derrick's mom comes to every one of his games at the United Center. Before each game begins, Derrick walks across the court to face her and blow her a kiss. "I love that," said his mom. "It makes my heart swell."

Derrick (#1) goes to the net against the Miami Heat's Dwyane Wade (#3) in 2011.

The Help of Others

Derrick's journey from Englewood to the NBA wasn't an easy one. People in his neighborhood faced crime and **poverty**. Often Derrick heard gunshots while playing ball. Although many Englewood kids got into trouble, Derrick never did. "My family sheltered me and made sure I stayed on the right path," he said. "I am lucky to have them in my life."

Family support is a key to Derrick's success. That's why today he works hard to support others and help them succeed. For example, Derrick bought backpacks for Englewood students who couldn't afford them. He also tries his best to be a role model to these kids by going back to the neighborhood to visit. "They're not used to seeing famous people or anybody around who's really successful," said Derrick. "I hope seeing me can drive them, because I know when I was younger, if somebody like me came back to the neighborhood, I would've made sure I remembered that day and I would want to be like that person."

Derrick's three brothers helped guide and protect him as he grew into a basketball star in Englewood.

In summer 2011, Derrick worked with **sponsors** to raise $20,000 to renovate the Murray Park basketball court. Now neighborhood kids get to play on a freshly painted court with new hoops.

Derrick works with some young players during a basketball camp that he hosted in 2009.

Far Away

Derrick also helps people who live far away from his hometown. When a terrible earthquake devastated Haiti in January 2010, he wanted to assist the people who had been affected by the disaster. "The season's going on . . . I couldn't make a trip over," said Derrick at the time. Yet he knew he could do something. As a result, he **pledged** to donate $1,000 to the Clinton Bush Haiti Fund for each point he scored in the game against the Phoenix Suns on January 22, 2010. He finished with 32 points, raising $32,000.

He repeated the pledge when an even bigger earthquake struck Japan in March 2011. This time he pledged $1,000 for each point he scored in the game against the Memphis Grizzlies on March 25, 2011. Derrick ended up with 24 points, raising $24,000 for a group that provided medical care to the Japanese disaster victims.

Here, Derrick scores against the Suns, earning another $1,000 for the Clinton Bush Haiti Fund, a charity started by former presidents Bill Clinton and George W. Bush to help the people of Haiti after the earthquake struck.

Derrick shoots during the game against the Memphis Grizzlies.

Derrick didn't just raise money with the points he scored against Phoenix and Memphis; he also helped the Bulls win games. Chicago beat the Suns, 115–104, and the Grizzlies, 99–96.

Aiming for Success

The Memphis and Phoenix games are probably the only two times that Derrick has ever given much thought to his own scoring. In most games, he is mainly concerned with helping his teammates score, and, of course, winning. In 2010–2011, his MVP season, he did plenty of both. After leading Chicago to 62 wins, he helped the Bulls defeat the Indiana Pacers and the Atlanta Hawks in the playoffs. The Bulls reached the Eastern Conference Finals, where they lost to the Miami Heat. Derrick hopes that one day he will lead the Bulls all the way to an NBA title.

No one knows if Derrick will achieve his ultimate goal with the Bulls. One thing is certain, however. Chicago fans will continue to enjoy watching one of the NBA's greatest point guards. They will also get to know a person who is very dedicated to two tasks— helping his teammates on the court and helping others off the court.

Derrick goes up for a shot in the playoff game against the Hawks in 2011.

In 2009, Derrick worked with the Greater Chicago Food Depository. This organization helps feed hungry people in Chicago by distributing food to those who can't afford it. Derrick appeared in advertisements to help people learn more about the group.

Derrick talks to some kids during a holiday party in 2010.

The Derrick File

Derrick is a basketball hero on and off the court. Here are some highlights.

 When Derrick was two years old, one of his favorite activities was sitting on his brothers' basketball and rocking back and forth. His brothers would tell him to stop, and Derrick would start to cry. Finally, they got him his own ball.

 In 2010–2011, Derrick was the only NBA player to finish in the top ten in both scoring and assists.

 During his MVP season, Derrick became the fifth player in NBA history to have at least 2,000 points, 600 assists, and 300 **rebounds**. Only four other players—LeBron James, Oscar Robertson, John Havlicek, and Michael Jordan—have ever done that before.

accurate (AK-yuh-ruht) on target

agile (AJ-uhl) able to move gracefully, quickly, and easily

All-Star (AWL-*star*) a player chosen to compete in a game in which the best NBA players from the East Coast play against the best NBA players from the West Coast

assists (uh-SISTS) when a player makes passes that set up his or her teammates to make baskets

commissioner (kuh-MISH-uh-nur) a person in charge of a department or organization

draft (DRAFT) an event in which professional teams take turns choosing college athletes to play for them

driving (DRIVE-ing) moving rapidly while dribbling the basketball

Eastern Conference (EES-turn KON-fur-*uhnss*) one of two 15-team divisions making up the NBA

FIBA World Championship (ef-eye-bee-AY WURLD CHAM-pee-uhn-*ship*) an international basketball tournament, in which countries compete against one another

foul (FOWL) an action, such as hitting someone, that goes against the rules of the game

humble (HUHM-buhl) not boastful about one's abilities or achievements

humility (hyoo-MIL-uh-tee) not being too proud; the awareness of one's faults

NCAA Championship Game (en-see-ay-AY CHAM-pee-uhn-*ship* GAME) the game that determines college basketball's champion team

outside shooting (OUT-side SHOOT-ing) attempting shots a long distance away from the basket

pledged (PLEJD) promised

point guard (POINT GARD) the basketball player whose main jobs are to run plays and pass the ball to teammates who are in a position to score

poverty (POV-ur-tee) being very poor

rebounds (REE-boundz) balls that are caught by a player after a missed shot

recruit (ri-KROOT) to persuade an athlete to attend a college and play for its sports teams

rookie (RUK-ee) a first-year player

sponsors (SPON-surz) people or companies that use a player or celebrity to help advertise their products

titles (TYE-tuhlz) championships

Bibliography

Deveney, Sean. "Like a Diamond in the Sky." *Sporting News* (March 14, 2011).

Friedell, Nick. "Rose Gives to Haiti." ESPN.com (January 22, 2010).

Hamilton, Brian. "Ignorance Bliss for Blossoming Rose: Chicago Prep Star Just Discovering How Good He Truly Is." *Chicago Tribune* (July 19, 2006).

Read More

Caffrey, Scott. *The Story of the Chicago Bulls (The NBA: A History of Hoops)*. Mankato, MN: Creative (2011).

Howell, Brian. *Chicago Bulls (Inside the NBA)*. Edina, MN: ABDO (2012).

Woog, Adam. *Derrick Rose (People in the News)*. Detroit, MI: Lucent (2010).

Learn More Online

To learn more about Derrick Rose and the Chicago Bulls, visit
www.bearportpublishing.com/BasketballHeroes

Index

T 6404